FROM ACORN TO OAK

POETRY & PROSE
WRITTEN BY
EMILY WILLARD

SCISSORTAIL PRESS
Stillwater, Oklahoma

ISBN: 978-1-955814-65-2

Cover by Melissa Marie Triana & Emily Willard
Book design by Brian Fuchs

Scissortail Press
www.scissortailpress.com
4500 E Burris Rd
Glencoe, OK
74032
USA

To James for being the best partner in crime when it comes to parenting our beautiful children.

CONTENTS

* *a collaboration with Lisea Silvers*

FORWARD

It was on a poetry live on Instagram, I remember reading Emily for the first time. Her piece 'Into The Void' - a visceral telling of a trauma story had me in grips and choking through the very first syllables.

Her writing had such a sharp impact on me, I reached out to her afterward to compliment her on her writing and we got talking. A sharp memory amongst many in my mind and just as well, because that was the beginning of a lasting, loving, and meaningful friendship. How far Em and I have come since then, how deeply is she a part of my everyday existence, in less than a year that now feels like a lifetime.

I may be one of many admirers of her written word but there are many reasons why Em is special to me. A unique identity that stands out in the sea of writers. Em is emphatically IN LOVE with words. This is someone who writes every day, so whether that is 6 words or 600, there is an unmistakable believability in every syllable her pen breathes.

"A circle of oaks whispers the sacred secrets of the old faith, as I step barefoot into a place I've always known, in this life and the last.
Dewy dawn and peppermint tea warms welcomed life into morning cooled hands."

Lines like that constantly remind me of why she is so special and gifted. In as short as two lines, she has all my senses awakened and has me effortlessly transported into her world where I can SEE, FEEL, TASTE, AND TOUCH experiences almost in a way as if they might have been first hand.

Pieces like Summer Loving and Planted Hearts;

> *"I gaze into*
> *tangerine and pomegranate skies*
> *blanketing the horizon of burnt beige-*
> *green fields. Bracing breezes catch*
> *the underneath of tulip skirts and*
> *spread-out blushed petals for*
> *honeybees taking."*

are evoking reminders of Em's love, reverence, and deep connection with nature. Her passion is gifted to the reader in how she presents her words. Poetry becomes a physical and palpable experience.

And then in pieces like Fallen Relapse, Not Today and She Calls Me,

> *"I'm silent*
> *Throat closed and with nothing to say,*
> *constricted conversation conflicted*
> *rationalization silenced by my own*
> *inner baneful sermons, creating*
> *isolation with unread unanswered*
> *unavailability."*

Em shows you her tenderness and wisdom in the understanding of the human condition.

And she does all this while juggling various hats as a writer, a friend, a daughter, a sister, and as a mum to her beautiful children, Freya, Jack, Poppy, and Noah.

Turning the pages as you read is like getting acquainted very much with Em herself, her honesty, her empathy, and compassion. Reading her poetry is very much a whole life experience in pages and words.

Em's debut book is a must-have for every reader and writer of poetry. From acorn to oak will leave you feeling the same impact that I felt when I first read her. Her writing is beautifully contemplative and encourages you to have inner conversations with yourself. Whether you're looking to escape from the drudge of daily life or you're looking to find yourself, the following pages, will probably leave you both, spellbound and answered in your pursuit.

—Stuti Sinha
(IG: @weavingtapestry)

Acknowledgments

A few sprinkles of love to:

MY FRIENDS

Jenna and Ann for being patient and kind
while I explore this crazy life of becoming
a writer and perusing my dreams

THE POETS

Danny, for Always just believing in me.
Seeing me especially when I do not.
Robert Cozzi, for weaving magic into my
heart and seeing Love exactly like I do.
The Wonderful Stuti for blending your
mind with mine, and having the same
writing dance as I.

All at Soul Connection Poets
and
The Writers Guild

ERIK

my beloved heart mate and best friend,
for saving me from myself and helping
me love me again.

**MY CHILDREN
FREYA, JACK, POPPY AND NOAH**

They are the reason I am who I am and
they showed a kind of love that I never
knew existed....
MAGIC

POETRY

THE BREATH OF THE FOREST

A circle of oaks whispers the sacred secrets of the old
faith, as I step barefoot into a place I've always known.
In this life and the last.
Dewy dawn and peppermint tea warms welcomed life
into morning cooled hands.
Do you think they remember me?
I feel embraced by their outstretched limbs, their
waving leaflets greet me with woodsy familiarity.
My roots are buried amongst their own. Memories of
a younger self perched upon the very bough I tip toe
beneath now.
Oh, the things they must have seen.

Peace blooms blithesome in my aching mind as I speak
of what a year it's been.
I tip my lips at twittering reply of Blackbirds.
The Oak, always trusty and true coats my heart in the
earthy reminiscence, of a different life.
Times with friends some long since passed; Stepping
out cloaked in search for the magical Mistletoe.
Breathe in the gift of a given breath
Breathe out the tint of yesterday's woes.
Such joy to step into my happy place.
My giggle dances atop the leaves
While I wander beneath the trees.

WHAT SITS IN OUR CHESTS?

Hanging stares held in macrame garlands weaved with
the nested feathers of nightingales that accompany the
harmonies sung by our souls' connection.
Words and emotions dance their way between our eyes
Unspoken
Unneeded
Undeniable
Red thread gravitation pulls our branches towards
each other dancing in the canopies of the same trees
just in different woodlands.
Reaching longingly
Stretching fervently
Digging our roots deeper into wishing soil; pulling a
desired sustenance into what sits in our chests.
You.
Me.
Our heart.

DOOMS DAY

If the rest of the world
Should enkindle into nothing
But flames

Could we paint what should
Rise from the ashes my love?

For moments like ours
Are destined to shake up
all that is

My darling, would we be
Fools not to step
Into what has always been?

7TH NOVEMBER 2020

I wrote a poem about you today.
Then deleted it. Gone.
It made me cry, but not just tears of reminiscence, or
tears of longing. No.
The type of tears that fall like led, when you know
something will never be the same again.
Like crimson stains upon a new white t-shirt poured
from clumsy hands on a night out.
"us" will never be the same again.
Mourning the loss of 17 years.
For what?...

PERIWINKLE SOUL

Come on to the Ice.
Do you trust me?
Would you even care if it broke?
Lost in eyes cool as frozen amber, the sign of our times
means I'll leave content in your embrace. Calamity is
now stitched into the underside
Of my skin, scratching at the surface not quite sure if I
want to release it or pull it in.
Head filled with "humumbles" rummaging around my
brain.
Tap. Tap. Tap.
Ice pick lobotomy's scream for Sandy lands.
Sand is overrated. It's just tiny, little rocks.
So go....
No. I don't want to you to.
Now evenly spaced
Now arms spread out;
Distribution perfect so we don't fall
THEN

You pull me closer. CLEMENTINE scents fill your
lungs as you inhale my essence from the side of my

neck.
Just
below
the
earlobe.
CRACK
 I feel you hold me closer.
CRACK
 My soul Is feeling complete
Crack
You get up and run: away from me, leaving me.
Vulnerable and exposed to the bitter elements;
Sunshine eternally shining on my bitter deathbed as
you make the shore.
Pulling Pushing
Pulling Pushing
I need to feel the freeze

Put out the fire from letting you in.
I call out. Not pained, or hurt.
No; in a beautifully sad way.
 I call his name.

"Please, take this", I reach inside of my mouth and with a regurgitated stretch I pull her out.
Her aura was almost blinding, though small, she would be seen for miles. Periwinkle shone from its core. And just seeing it, no longer with me sewed guttural grief into my sternum. But it was where it belonged. With him…she would be happy there.

"Please take this. I don't need it anymore"
CRACK
This is me.
This is my stop.
Our fire extinguished by the ice you abandoned me on.
Numb and withdrawn I am inhaled by the river and breathe at one with the Gaer now
He holds my soul cradled in his hands gently strokes it and whispers 'it's going to be okay'
Turns around and walks away.

He whispers to the wind
"Meet me at that place we spoke about"

LEARN TO FLY

Sometimes having your
world ripped from beneath
your feet isn't as bad as it
first may seem

Because its then you must
learn to fly.

It's all about perspective

Memory Book

Press my heart like flowers
Into the dog-eared memories
You save for rainy days

ℙLANTED 𝕃IPS

As our lips met.
Seeds were planted
Causing an instant bloom
To rise from my throat
Now they wilt and curl
In wait to flourish
At just a small press
Of your tongue.

HUNGRY

I am starving,
A starvation only satiated by the touch of my star
The one the universe deemed impossible for me to be
with
I am hungry
I am hungry
I am hungry
Universe on blinded knees
I hold my eye in the palms of my hand for you to gift
me freedom
Freedom from him
Freedom from my love
Freedom from my sight
Take this tie and hang me with it, for if it not be him
then loneliness calls my name and I refuse to follow
him home

WINGED STARS

Tasting winged stars excavated from my chrysalis core
as they take flight in my smiling sighs; finding their
home in the same night sky. A safety blanket vast
enough to envelop us both. You are a babbling brook
nourishing my earth and nurturing a nursery of new
adoration we have for ourselves and each other. My
earth holds space for you to run fluidly and paint
warm permanence into the season we always belonged
to.
A place.
For you
For me
For us
To just be.

MESSAGE

Ding. Phone. News.
Rooted to the spot; my heart pounds forcing congealed
crimson through weary veins. My mind a Helter-
skeleta of nothing and everything burying lucidity
replacing it with execrable hostility. Violent chest
convulsions rain blows to my lungs till a "pop pop"
sound awakens at my sternum.
Swallowing air like I'm thirsty for life all whilst
pleading to myself to just embrace its finality. The over
dramatics of my mind manifesting just one message,
into the complete obliteration of peace. Finally
Holding in that last heave clinging to my rib cage.
Time to say goodbye
Time to end the pain
Time to put out the flames
Time to follow my inevitability

Times UP

Eyes rolled up then back; forcing heavy lids into their
assent; rationale sweeps silk across shards of
uncertainty and choked breaths fill my lungs as light
pierces my gaze bringing clarity to my thoughts.

I am ok.
I am safe.
I am not alone.
I am alive.
Breathe
Breathe
Breathe
Breathe.

Three agonising minutes feels like a lifetime in the
grips of anxiety. Especially when you are alone.

ꓦALLEN RELAPSE

I am bruised
Blue black blood vessels creep into bolt lightning
tantrums tainting my discorded mind, fading into
mouldy greens of discontent and angry mauves of
indignation. Kissed by unsolicited trauma with no ice
pack in sight.

I am depleted
My light has all but dimmed to a barely blinking led
bulb upon a switchboard buried inside a long outdated
90s video game, unwanted useless, positivity discarded
deep within a box long forgotten.

I am contorted
Violently twisted thoughts bend their way into a half
healed holistically harnessed gallery of open hope,
creating a manger knot dripping in wolf's bane
creeping toxicity Into my limbic system.

I'm silent
Throat closed and with nothing to say, constricted
conversation conflicted rationalisation silenced by my
own inner baneful sermons, creating isolation with
unread unanswered unavailability.

I'm hurting
All over, mind, body spirit and sundered soul lost in a

realm of uncertainty and listless sleep, psychological war zones birth swollen clouds of seismic myodynia, crippling all that is me in a blast wave destroying my weakened vessel

I'm deprived
Of human interaction but a stagnant contradiction because I shelter in my own bubble of supersaturated solitary, unable to burst forth into an ever craved embrace.

I'm defeated
Sucked of oxygen and buoyancy; death greats me like a discarded foil birthday balloon hanging from the neck of an oak in an uncharted woodland. Painfully unexisting, unseen and unheard with no suicide net to catch my fated fall

I am lost
Someone come find me
Follow the trail of fallen promise
As I drag my weathered veins across battered grounds.
Scratched into the barkless trunk of a tree long torn from life will be the map to my light.
Etched with sharpened shards snapped from my wrists for what is written in bone finds more permanence than the pen.

LOST LOVE

She finds her return home in the noiseless heart of
dawn, after unceasingly searching for the keeper of
souls.

Calling for her mirrored self she seeks solace in her
night, for there is always light amidst the
shadows, reflecting off the moon.

Abandoned by fickle paramours, no longer willing to
give her love freely; her heart listens for its song in the
wind beneath the stars. Somewhere between their sea
and hers is a boundless love hanging in wait for it's
harmonised pair.

Some say, night hides life's truths but not she, her
witness of the day sees it's masks slipping and finds
clarity under the noir abyss. With a throat packed with
moon beam She spews light onto the boundless
blanket of darkness to guide her heart home.

Emily Willard

Summer Loving

Dipping my honey drenched lips into the festooned pupil of a storm filled teacup, feasting on the warm nectar of the goddess Hesperides; I gaze into tangerine and pomegranate skies blanketing the horizon of burnt beige-green fields. Bracing breezes catch the underneath of tulip skirts and spread-out blushed petals for honeybees taking. Twilight heat still warms close air; summer hugging alone with a bag of food and tea makes for an evening of dreams. Midsummer nights like these rise a lust within me that seeps from my pores. A sensual sky and sugar dipped fruit flick a switch that coats my mind in seductive ambrosia. I run my middle finger slowly down my face, starting from my sweat drenched brow to the tip of my chin, rolling my head back as the decent ends. Senses spring to life. Eyes drowning in hues of sunset painted skies. Nose filled with the sweet scents of fruit, and dried cut grass, ears filled with nightingales' songs and cricket's violin solos played just for me. I lay back upon the grass and take one deep and desperate breath. Trying to Inhale the memories of this day, I say goodnight to the sun before I pack myself up and begin to wonder home barefoot underneath Luna and her Twinkling companions, feeling in that moment with a lazy smile falling from my face.

Perfectly infinite.

Emily Willard

A Tale of Becoming

When I look at her.
Like really look at her I am in awe of her resplendent
beauty.
The way my body reacts to her lopsided smile is
nothing Short of sorcery. The flush to my skin makes
me question if she has seen-what a simple gesture does
to my face.
Sat here in a field with a few of our friends; Drinks
flowing freely- teenage debauchery at its finest,
Alcohol seems to be taking effect as I can't seem to
take my eyes off of her. The way she rolls her head
back whilst lying in the Sun; catches me of guard. We
are surrounded by people; can they see me? it doesn't
matter because I cannot take my eyes from her delicate
collarbones; Wondering what her skin would feel like
against a small press of my tongue
Enthralled by the lobes of her ears, eyes fixed on the
patch of tightly stretched flesh just below.
that bare,
soft,
silky....

What was wrong with me? why am I looking at my friend like this? it must be the booze. And then- she laughs; like this laugh that erupts from her core, it's loud and it's melodic and it's delightful and; oh my gosh am I thinking about her laugh. Yes; yes, I am because at that moment one million butterflies take flight in my stomach and I melt. Tears filling the edges of my blue orbs; looking at her blue orbs thinking wow I've never seen them like that before, as blue as the sea is in Perranporth Bay, and when she catches my eye, they turned stormy. She had seen me; she has known that I've been looking at her all day.
Her entire being Oozed sensuality in a way that was sumptuous and sexy.

Then something clicked, like bugs crawling all over my body, the hot flush warming my cheeks turned to glass shards of shame.
The butterflies dispersed and-my head dropped. I turned away as my body lolled in embarrassment.
Years later, still haunted by the memories of that day I

realised what she had done to me. She had lit the fire
inside of me; the fire that made me feel like I was
different.
Sometimes it made me feel broken.
sometimes it made me feel perverse.
sometimes it made me feel like I just wanted to
disappear and I threw myself at every man that I
could. Just to prove myself; my brain this isn't who I
was. Now reflecting on that day, I realised it wasn't her
that played with sorcery. it was me all along, because I
could see a soul for soul; they shone out like an aura,
not based on
their race or their gender or anything other than their
soul; and they burned bright to me like a beacon
drawing me in; Moth to a flame I Revelled in the
beauty of people smiles
people's eyes
People bodies
and Peoples laughs.
because I fall in love with people.
I now know, that's ok.

Emily Willard

HOME COMFORTS

Comfort is when I can hear
the trees whisper their
secrets to the breeze. I will
always dig my roots into soil
never too far from a
woodland. Making sure we
can share the Earth and
grow in unison: being
framed by their beauty.
Now that's my hearts home.

ꆜLLUSION OF ꆜOVE

It is the ultimate emotional mirage,
Blindsided by seductive untruths,
The bone China organ held with slippery fingertips,
Naively unprepared for its inevitable fracture,
Vulnerability is its unadorned target,
Tainting your sight and moulding rose coloured orbs,
Splendidly mendacious in its sadistic assault,
The nocuous illusion of love.

Emily Willard

WHEN WILL BE THE LAST?

My darling Noah

You are nearly 10 and my heart cracks open every time that age plays on loop in my mind. There is something so very sad about those double figures. The finality of your baby years feels like a loss I haven't felt before. Strangely, it's not something that was present when the other three children hit your age. I mean I was a little glum, but I was excited for them to be growing up and leaning into that new chapter in life. With you it's different, you are my last. The last of many things and the loss is undeniable. No, It's pitifully unbearable. The day you were born I knew we were finished. Our family was complete. We were all perfectly content. One whole year later, almost to the day, it all came crashing down from the pedestal I had us held on. The home you, your brother and sisters had shared became a barren wasteland, and was trying to kill me.

Eating me from the inside out. That part of me that had protected you while you grew was taken away from us in an emergency. From me. Discarded like an

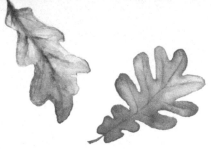

out-of-date beef joint, pungent and putrid it was
rushed to the bin before anyone could even think
about how much it costs or all the potential it could
have had, and how it made the family full. That loss
itself was hard to recover from, I am still in mourning
for the vessel I called my own, but I knew no matter
what, all would be okay, because I had my babies. I
had you. Last week you brushed my kiss off of your
cheek, and said "Mum, I'm not a baby anymore"
when I held your beautiful face, our eyes locked for a
few seconds and no words needed to be said, you
rolled your eyes and giggled and then ran off to play.
Those silent words spoke themselves.

I often wonder about your "lasts". The last time you
will willingly reach your little palm up to mine with
even thinking while walking through the supermarket.
How you subconsciously rub your tiny thumb up and
down the side of my Index finger. It's like year-round
Christmas morning feelings flutter from my heart at
the simple gesture. Even writing it now a single tear
sits on this page, memorialising what will soon be a
Kodak moment in your memory box. I think of the
last time you lean your little blonde head on my

shoulder and say "I love you Mummy" for no other reason than it's how you feel at that moment, pure unfiltered love. That right there is better than any feeling in the world. That word, Mummy, my gifted name when I became a parent, as if they themselves weren't enough I gave birth to a new identity and that name, will have a last time too.

There will be a day, and exact moment in time when those extra letters escape from your soft little lips. Then as if erased from your ever-growing vocabulary I evolve into "Mum" and I will never be known as Mummy again. Then, there will be the last time that you run out of school, big beaming smile on your face and take a running jump into my arms because you haven't seen me for six whole hours. All the other mums look at your daily welcoming ritual and it's what makes life worth living for. I am your world there is no denying that, but one day you will walk out of school talking to your friend, hand me your bag and walk off without even saying hello. That will be it, I will no longer be the centre of your world. I have no choice but to make room for others. For your growth and that hurts, hurts so good. That you have found courage to move on without me.

I will hold you extra tight my glacier eyed boy. With a soul that mirrors mine, and a mind so beautifully emotional and gentle. I will wake you at night and sneak you into my bed just to see your smile at us being up late, chatting away about feelings, poetry and lord of the rings. Keeping my eyes closed in the mornings even when awake, just to be woken with a little shake and a "Mummy, can you make me some Cheerio's!? Now please" and we will watch Pokémon till we are so hyped we walk and walk and walk just to hatch a Pokémon we already have. With excitement bursting out of your ears I will listen to you tell me about every episode of Ninjago that I have watched at least 26 times just so I see that light in your eyes, the spark in your soul.

I hope that this time Isn't your last. You are nearly 10 my boy. You have told me with that dimpled grin on your face that you are not a baby anymore....
But trust me when I say this, you will forever be my little chicken nugget.

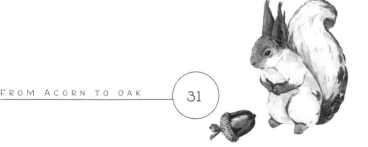

PLUCKED

As I run my fingers through
her tresses, I pluck the buds
and make her a crown

CLOUDS

Clouds fill with sadness
Feel my kisses in the rain
Carried in each loving drop

SHE CRIES

Crystalline rivers erode sorrow
Into the raised curves of Gaia's Garden.
Her heart's cry moves mountains, shaking in choked
desolation for her fallen kin, ripped from existence by
the life's she offers her giving breaths to.
Fossilised poison bleeds death into her veins
and the homes she birthed for communities, engulfed
in murderous flames.
How many more hours
How many more days

Will we continue to peel away her skin, feast on her
pulp and have the gall to complain she's gone bad?
Mother dear I will embrace you each day with a smile,
whisper to the next in line all the secrets to keep you
nourished.
Hold on please, I see something on your horizon.
I pray it's change.

CHINA CUPS

Bone china vulnerability seeps from protectively sewn
lips pulled out by kindness and unfiltered honesty; my
muscle mind space memories, dipped in fondness of
honeyed words, molten swallows' warm silken streams
as your tongue flicks and licks soft syllables from my
vocal cords. Spirits cloaked and exchanged in
delectable dopamine plumes. Magic surrounds you,
tell me where your secrets lie. Mystified merge collided
with all that is embedded in me; chest broken exposed,
labyrinth lost; reach in and pluck my bud from its stem
and watch it bloom in the palm of calloused hands.
Lie on your front bare yourself to me. I will tattoo
expression upon your skin; blinded by a light that
shines around you; feel me deep inside; new, rooted in
your cortex. Honeydew coats explorative extremities
composing the finale of my ultimate undoing.

Bedpost halos lost in a horned exchange; teeth sunken
into pomegranate sin spillers catching soft whispers of
a name I'm unable to hum.

CLOUD CHASER

Always mocked for having my head in the clouds,
dreaming big-to them unrealistic, to me I will be
enterally unsatisfied until I reach my final destination.
My views from up there, perspective and hindsight,
colours and the light blinding- inspiring undisturbed
content; unlike their energy. Lamentable making my
head heavy, negatively charged particles brewing up a
storm.
Creating darkness in my sunblind mind, a darkness
that I keep buried deep within me.
What was once drenched in the beauty of Borealis
now turned ashen, turmoil builds up until I become an
explosion of negative energy.
Lightening feed's my force back striking it victims with
no remorse, scorching them till there is no more than
burnt egos.
I dream of flesh being torn from their bones because
within the beauty of my mind there is also deep-
rooted madness.
Each strike a bullet cutting that cord of negativity
releasing me in charcoal hued plumes.
Clearing my skies, manifesting sunny days.
Sunflowers, trees and the turquoise seas drip back
through in twirls and swirls.
See, when my heads in the clouds, the best thing to do
is leave me alone. This side of me maybe a dreamer.
But clear skies are better than my deadly storms.

LIMBS OF TIME

Virtues cease to exist.

Static minds plunge into darkness.

You

Retreated and never came back.

Erased from your heart like I never held presence in
the first place.

Just a fly on the wall reaching in.

Destroying my opulent wings contorting my soul

Awakening a morning mist of sunless

skies.

Do you know what the branches see if you pay
attention?

Monumental absence, flexing distorted shadows
plucked from the birch hung over my already dug and
fated grave.

Pluck violets from my sparrow throat and lay them out
to season.

I shall tie bows around the limbs of time.

Pull them forward and Breathe in.

For days spent with a shattered star is like living life for
no reason.

SEA GLASS

Evergreen stems protrude from the cracks forged
across marrowless ribs; thorned arms blossom
from seeds planted in an echoing rotted cavity long left
for dead. I, was pulled in to Gaia's embrace; opened
by your giving mouth
as you spat your salve into festered wounds tainted by
living regret…..
Step by step
I played your love on healing repeat

You
licked my death wish clean with tongues dipped in
unfettered forgiveness

You
Stroked my suicide note and combed out the fatal
letters till they transformed into poetry

You
Kissed my paranoia on the forehead, looked me dead
in the eyes and said " always good enough"

You
Whispered my name three times into the face of

uncomfortable untruths; then went to war to find the
stone our destiny was set in.

With hands splayed across my sternum

You
Began CPR

We
Survive the deception of cravens;
Stand strong in storms of weathered Malevolence

We
Are not stitched together by fate to allow the
humdrums of human emotion bury us in my dark
corners.
You cooed new life into my wilted soul with each push
of adoration

Breathe in, breathe out
Breathe in, breathe out

Your canopy hangs deliberately and grants shade to
my longing; shielding vulnerable saplings from

artificial summers.
Feel my prose hummed into the ears of blackbirds as
they twitter our love language in-
Je vous aime les mélodies.

I tell the trees your name
Their leaves giggle

Atrium eyes, windows to his cumulus soul
Always on mine, as I twirl and spin pollinating
evermore. I dance like no soul is watching, charming
sweet periwinkle faces just for you.
You are green sea glass found on my forest floor.
So far from home but your vibrancy seduces the norm
to cast human limitations to the wind. Our woodlands
place their roots into the eyes of time needles and we
are threaded into a permanent existence.
Two hearts
Bleed into
One home
The trees lean in at the sound of your name and
whisper my secrets to the wind, for they know
You, have always been my favourite poem

DROWING AT SEA

Breathe in
Purge out.
Curdled coughs bubble from a throat desperate to rid
the imprint of his tongue that had tattooed its way
down my esophagus. Sleep evaded and scarred retinas
cake crackled cinema replays under weighted lids.
PTSD fucks sunshine days into next tuesdays and sews
storm clouds; needle pointed thunderstorms woven
into the crown of my cranium creating catastrophic
damage to any source of light.

Breathe in
Purge out.
Gauzy sails dawned on a ship destined for the most
violent of seas. My voyage was always fated to meet a
deep claret void in these oceans, purely to rub salt into

wounds of self harm and disfiguration. Forcing the
forever open tares to sting, my trauma? Identity crisis
ownership forcing the smiles and okays from chapped
lips and ulcerated cheek innards from a permanent
bile coated tongue.

Breathe in
Purge out.
Severed ties, and corrupted bonds force separation of
the true loved ones. Penetrated paranoia permeates
prickles in parental voices. Words drizzle into
damaged drums and metamorphose into toxicity. Love
translates to judgement. Little pill pots filled with
chemical charisma create artificial peace on those slick
filled; him drenched. seasons, until my blinking light
recharges and eventually refills my parched cups of
hope once again.

HIGH ON LIFE

My heart never stood a chance, with a mind that could
romanticize the death of a fly, spun by silk in a tomb
of unknowing; a comfortable farewell offering for the
mother spider and her kin. Rose coloured glasses bring
a glow to the life cycle of despair.

You know that saying, "she's got thick skin?" Well
mines membranous like a bat's wing. Deeply affected
by the woes of the world: losing sleep over the trauma
of strangers witnessed in the pages of history, or
screened on TV.

I get a kick over the beauty of words; shudder at their
curves and each syllable makes me sing. The verse bled

from the pen poured out of a writer's heart, forever
transporting me to their minds through their art.

Some may say I have an old soul: full of Grace and
forgiveness only matched by a loving mother; truth is
tending to the wound inflicted by others has become a
thing of beauty now. grudges keep wounds fresh and
leaves scars of regret.

The moral of my heart speaks this; you can only
spread disruption with embers of hate, being sure to
burn yourself on wildfires of animosity. Bathe in the
pools of colour and light. Watch your world transform
into a sea of delight.

BABY'S BREATH

I'll pick the bones in my chest
and fill it with baby's breath.
Pollenate my soul with
dandelion wishes
Plant daisies in every space you
hurt.

In 2020 I Fell in Love

I fell in love this year.
With someone that swept me off my feet
Pulling me out of the Lazarus pit and giving life to the
girl I hadn't seen in over a Decade.
My love fixed my broken pieces and held them
together with a clay that absorbed their whole heart
and sacred desires with each touch, painting those
broken pieces in the art of Kintsugi, Gold.
When I looked in the mirror today,
I saw something spectacular in my reflection, Unable
to really look at myself for years without seeing
something ugly and damaged beyond repair, I now see
the beauty through my love's eyes.
This human showed me a power inside her that
manifests the strength of an iceberg and its ability to
remain

strong and tall in the darkest of oceans
A heart that could love so hard that it could fill a room
of ice with its warmth
A mind so complex in a labyrinth type beauty, I'm lost
and there I want to stay
This person I will hold on to as if her very presence is
giving me life, breathing air into my lungs and
pumping the blood coursing through my veins.
Looking into the mirror staring at the person I fell in
love with a barely recognisable, yet wondrous woman,
I will forever love this version of myself.

NIGHT

Sleep deprived, she begins to wonder if she was a
creature of the night.
Born into darkness, folded inside the septic depth of
almighty sin.
cursed to reside inside inky black skies.
Sunlight brings a time in which she feels dead inside,
existing in the form of a stagnant skin suit.
Wasting away each day she'd pray for its power to
grant her solace, instead it's not until Its tendrils of
tangerine hues crawl into descension, the skies turn
noir; alongside the Nightingale's song her mind comes
to life.
Insomnia, now embraced as her closest companion
after years of trying to suppress her fate with
chemicals that tore the life out of her in turn.

Stripping her feelings bare, fabricating an
unrecognisable version of herself.

No.

she knew that wasn't the answer, she learned to accept
her fate.

Born nocturnal; has its perks.

Unafraid of what was lurking in the shadows, the stars
in the sky became her friends, she carried
constellations around her neck as a medal, and knew
the Moon's moods like she did her own; she revelled in
its power feeding her creativity, like an Astro butterfly-
she could spread her wings, mind flying with the stars.

Born into a curse of darkness, she bought her own
light in her poems, spilling black ink of her night onto
white pages of her day.

RAIN

Rain leaks built up tension
from darkened skies
I have always felt a caressed
connection with our mother
So much so
That even the weather
dances with my mind
Today my ducts ill with the
mottled horizon

HER STORMS

With a mouth full
of thunder,
She pulled the
summer from
his eyes,
Licked her lips,
And filled them
with her storm

FALLEN REGRET

Falls like
Desolate riverbanks
Stolen time
Creeps back

MIRRORED SOUL

There is no side of me he does not know,
yet does not love regardless.
Matchstick ribcage ignited by a gentle
flickered flame, seducing the cosmic beats
of a crimson star, Bourne of pure
porcelain light.
Forever refracted off of his mirrored soul

A Letter to My 15 Year Old Self

Hey Emily
It's Em.

I just wanted to let you know.
That everything is going to be ok.
And I know that's a cliche. but I mean it. Up until this
point you have done good girl.
High five!
But know, things are tough.
It's been hard to stay alive. But here you are.
I want to wrap one arm around you, and with the
other, stroke your hair and tell you, on Those nights
when you feel nothing but despair
"It's going to be ok. Everything will be fine"
You will smile, more than you cry.
You will laugh more than you want to die.

Things will feel heavy. No. No no.
Things will BE heavy.
But it's not the be all.
End all of your life anymore.
And you will feel.

Some days, like the ground is being ripped from beneath your feet.
But you will rise. Like a burning pyre destroying everything that stands in its way.
Just to keep moving.
To give out your love
And

  Be

    Loved

      In

       Return

There won't be many people in this world to see you or really feel you.
But there WILL BE a few.

It will take a while to find them. Sure. But they are there.
And they really really see you. Now that feeling right there?

    Is fucking beautiful.

The freest your soul will ever feel is when it's united

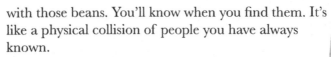

with those beans. You'll know when you find them. It's like a physical collision of people you have always known.

Except you haven't....   Or have you?

The bitterness won't last forever. I promise. And I know that shit stings. But trust me when I say.....

Something will fall into place.

Around the age of 32

And it's gonna Rock your world!

Everything that has happened.

Everything that is yet to come will lead to that day: a day where it all pieces together and just makes sense.

You are on the right path "Blue".

You will know LOVE.

In ways you cannot even comprehend.

It won't be the love you're expecting.

No - it's better than that.

YOU WILL KNOW LOVE OF YOURSELF.

One day you will look in the mirror

And no longer allow yourself to be a victim.

You will forgive yourself.

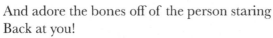

And adore the bones off of the person staring
Back at you!
A couple of practicalities…. If you get this…
Pink ISN'T YOUR COLOUR! don't bother dying
your hair that way!
Stay the hell away from Kiwi…. it will straight up try
and kill you.
Oh and remember these dates…..
4th March 2006
29th March 2007
11 September 2010
14th December 2011……

These are days that will save your life.
Enjoy.

I love you Emily.
Not always…. but from now and forever.

Em

SOLARIS SUNSHINE

Summer mornings blending night into day a Solaris oil painting hangs on to a nightingale canvas; faintly splattered with star freckles now bidding farewell to a wearied moon. Dripping luminescent light across the lids of our cerulean and pecan eyes slowly ascending in our daily awakening ritual.

The crisp caress of the baby's breath lifts the closed skirts of delicate daisies dotting shamrock Meadows; shaking awake the sleeping bees. Stirring them into unfurled morning melodies. Impelling us to take thirsty gulps of each other, drinking in the essence of a blessed new day.
The rising warmth hugs the air closer as the day

awakens, Lullabies dance into the harmonies of rhyme and prose swathed in piquant sorcery. I roll back my head to the plum seeds of passion planted upon my neck. Nodding an echo to each petal crowned atop verdant stems as they are kissed by the star of light.

Sweet Orchid Inhalation fills my petals with a dewy coating as his hummingbird tongue sips sticky nectar. calling sunshine showers and arched bows in elated symphonies. Knowing lips tip as breathy sighs escape our chests. Like in hourglass retreat we lassoed back to the first dawn of our love. The tambourine shakes of leaves on trees overwhelm senses and we are lost in a sweet nostalgic nirvana.

19ᵀᴴ JUNE 2021

You say you loved your eyes.
Especially the way they look
when the sun catches
them....

I instantly smiled.
Because, yea. I do too.

SKY KISSES

When the sky kisses your skin with
wet lips
We have a choice to hide from its
embrace. Or stand in place and be
watered for growth.
I was made to feed this earth.
I will forever embrace all that she
hands me.

Emily Willard

Fated Stars

There aren't many stars that
do not hold our name.
But we will press our fated
hearts into the ones that
don't.

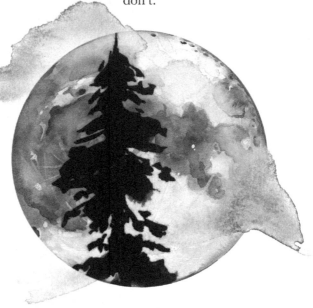

TALKING TO THE MOON

Have you seen my moon?
She waits for me
Each passing night.
Star crossed and surrounded,
Hung in a cosmos clothesline
She is my greatest listener

Have you seen my moon?
Her face, so bewitching
She seduces the
Seas to the sands.
A siren's song held
In a star freckled sky

Have you seen my moon?
I tell her all about you.
Of a human with a heart that parallels
Mine, and a soul that loves her like I do,
I look up in wonder

Do you tell her of me?
Because of course
She is your moon too.

SHE CALLS ME

I like to flirt with death.
I'll perch on the edge of towered roofs and watch the
skies burn molten embers with lemonade hues, one
nudge and my free-falling bones will shatter into
shards of elated expiration.

My dormant doormat body springs to life in
adrenaline junkie highs, the heated rush of driving so
fast butterflies take flight. Cackled laughter explodes
from my throat as the world surrounding me turns to a
smudged oil painting, the only constant is I.

I dance and sing in thunderstorms of crackling light
and stinging rain. Repetitive rumbles ricochet through
my core and each CRACK births tingles across my
skin. Fear and desire hum the same tune into my eager
ears. Petrichor mixed with battery acid lines my mind
with blind excitement

When I'm falling in faster than I breathe. Each slither
of my heart I offer to another soul, takes part of my
life bringing me closer to the edge each time it's

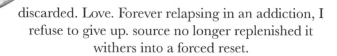

discarded. Love. Forever relapsing in an addiction, I refuse to give up. source no longer replenished it withers into a forced reset.

I've danced with the devil and been baptised of my sins. Only for my human vessel to break those unblessed vows again and again. Red spider Lily lamentation forces fistfuls of a poisoned wake into an already slowing heart.

I do not fear death, She welcomes me into a warm embrace. Her finality seductively draws me under with hypnotic harmonies; I sway and wait with baited breath.
I fear a life unlived
I fear a life unloved
I fear a life unfulfilled

I have died a thousand times, this season is all but a pebble in an estuary lying in wait for something more, in the next wave carrying me into the oceans of a new life

FALLEN SACRIFICE

Garnet sisters upon her face, pomegranate secret
spillers shush for the right price. Hips, hourglass
weapons of mass destruction; swaying to the beat of
seductions drums. Hypnotic melodies seep from her
throat, into the ears of the patsy she's laid eyes upon.
She rolls her tongue around tasteless consequence and
bathes in belligerently brittle shame; Come hither eyes
fixate on every woman's man, a pick and mix of silk
lined pockets she will crawl inside of until her skins
turned green.

She bows for her heckling audience. You see; this
creature of the night was a callous crafter of future
regret. A Salacious stealer of souls empty of virtue, on
a quest from her master to find new recruits. She picks
seven sins from the crowns of her teeth and wears
them hanging off a chain around her neck. Each a
Medal of Honour as she looks on with contentment
resentment at the murder of birds spread out for her
taking.

See, the stumps where her wings once sat; now
decorated with the blood of her suitors. An abiding
reminder that she no longer belongs in the light and
the tenebrosity is now her bedfellow. She traded her

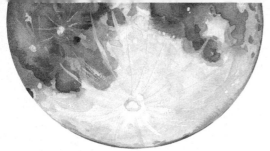

last kiss with light for the soul of her son, he was eight years old when evil tainted his blood supply; stripping his Vibrant colour and replacing it with mottled grey. The trade was like heaven itself and one she lapped up like a thirst in the Sahara; with no time to even look back.

He would live on.

He would love on.

He breathe on.

She would continue with pleasure to rip the cords on lives unknown and smile her Cheshire grin to awaken the hibernating lips of the pure bloods, and feed their souls to the dark. Then slip into a baby like slumber, seeing the eyes of her one true love living in her dreams. Blizzard blue lenses; the ones that were etched into her mind, greet her each night with open arms. Her shaped face upon a frail boned boy framed with golden curls capture her heart and obliterates the blackness that crawls inside of her. They play and pray as she personifies the light that she once was. Passing up words of hope to all and every deity that may listen, that she could remain sewn into the tapestry of bliss, with the light of her life.

Little Sparrow

You plucked each feather one by one from the broken wings of the sparrow like bird found in the hollows of your walls. Using the end of one as a toothpick memorial that would stay hidden in your draw till the day I left. Jars of sun bathed tears remained stored on your sill as a sadistic reminder that you had to twist just a little and these eyes would spill the secrets of a burned out soul. Crouching carcasses crippled with crimson crowns were your favourite play things; I needed out before the throne was passed to me an unfair maiden of a victims reborn vessel. Purple fist kisses painted this once pristine yet pale canvas and what a sight I was to behold. Your work of art hung to dry in a gallery of potentially fatal consequence. Your absence was the silent solace; air filling weary lungs and a numbness I grew beautifully comfortable with.

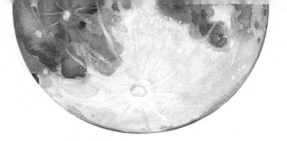

Till one day I opened that draw.

One single sparrows feather lay on its bottom. I reached out and curled trembling fingers around the brittle quill. As if the spirit of the sparrow coursed through my veins and entire broken being, my wings grew strong; breaking through battered skin; bringing a non-human strength that set me free; off I flew. Never looking back and only following the wind as it whispered my name. Constantly calling keeping me permanently moving. Forever escaping from the collector of hearts encased in that darkest of rooms.
Sometimes I hear the painful echo's of my name called by you; little liquid lullabies lulling me to sleep knowing the pain of losing me will haunt you till your days end.

Emily Willard

FROM ACORN TO OAK

STUTI

She walks with me.
Hands linked and fingers entwined, we tiptoe, in silent
knowing. Across uncharted lands, baron of our own
blooms, planting seeds into each other's gardens.
Patiently holding on in wait for lavender fields of love
to coat our skin and noses, birthing beauty in numb
darkness. She weaves tendrils of warmth creating
intricate tapestries in my tall walls. And outpouring of
grace blows in from the east and settles upon a heart in
the west. Magical melodies from angelic lungs fill
wanting ears burying sounds of tears and filling them
with harmonies of hope. When her voice loses sound,
I fill it with mine. Adoration affirmations of tangible
truths fill empty spaces lying in wait to be swallowed
refilling empty chords, so my sleeping angel can sing
once more.

Emily Willard

I Love Me

Today I chose to forgive
myself
I shed her skin and walked
away from the remains, into
a form unknown, but true to
who she always was
I climbed the wall and
looking into new beginnings
through glacier eyes
Tipped my lips and told her
"I love YOU"

Emily Willard

CONSUME

We consume what we adore,
and I am incessantly satisfied
with the spread laid out
before me.

NAKED ATTRACTION

There are these Lilac eyes that draw the ability to
undress my soul. Nights spent gazing into those
penetrating pools dismantle any nocturnal woes,
replacing them with an entire soul bonding and
Amethyst showers. He stole back my tears; the ones I
had been drowning in for what felt like forever;
creating an epoch in the study of my mind. Selflessly
teaching me that my soul is something to be marvelled
at, and that even if I am ever alone. I will never really
be lonely; for his soul is branded into my heart and the
point of Cupid's arrow has scratched his name into my
bones, scribing; him and I- true love always. Blue
Morpho Butterflies reside permanently in my core
taking flight every time I see you through my minds
eye; skipping through my daydreams he takes
perpetual residence in my psyche and I wilfully
handed over the key. His stare, matching mine; always
hungry.

VIRGO AND ARIES

A flame burnt inside of an earthy soul
drenched in bitter darkness and ignited a force within
her that bought life to a land that was considered long
baron.

An elemental collision of a poet's kind turned into two
halves of the same whole.
A sense of longing aches inside of our hearts, sisters
in this world and forced apart.

HIS AND HER STORY TO TELL

As I lay down with you, wrapped in sheets of linen; I
hum you name with no sound because you hear the
caress in my mind without me needing to part my lips.
Rhapsodic realisation sings harmonies into my
hallowed halls of tainted amor.
The way you lick my scars and heal my wounds with
whispered lullabies dissolves each millilitre of doubt
dimpled into my guarded walls.
Until a shadow casts over and dims your light,
Twisted typhoons of tepid temptation create havoc on
a mind built only for sunny weather.
"i'm sorry darling I don't feel you anymore"
Wait
Don't go....
Bubbled breaths fall from a choked throat, deep
starless night sets into blooming cracks, diminishing all
life buddling from old wounds.
That feeling.
A tangible entity.
Dull razor blades scraping against soft skin.
You were gone.
Banished from my mind by the sharded deep sapphire

sorrow of your blackened soul.

Gulping cried weave into my core reaching into my oesophagus in creeping grief.

Gone.

Obsidian obliterated my vision, consuming any light of the dream that danced in my wake.

The grief.

The fucking grief, built and built so high till I felt like all I could do was break apart.

Sour bile coated my tongue and any brief sense of stability was severed as I came undone.

Your eyes.

A green that teetered on the edge of meadowed hues seen only in the birth of spring and fresh wands of grass. Washed away from my mind by the oceans busting in reaction to this everyday-mare now cross stitched into my forever fate.

Your said "goodbye."

I said "go to sleep."

You did.

But never woke.

IGNITE MY LOVE, IGNITE

A spark ignited in a guarded heart. Dripping lyrical
aloe onto welted memories.
Basking in muted moments; hypnotised in gentle eyes
cradled in the soft amour of unspoken, loudly heard
truths.
Greeted by the wombed light of a new born love
supply, hummingbird beats flutter and whistle through
my open ribcage; healing heart harmonies sing for my
mirrored soul.
My softness builds hardness and my rawness
contradicts all that encompasses me.

Emily Willard

PSA

In a world choked by the
kings and queens of
fabrication.
Light fires of subtle
destruction in the
conversations adorned by
patriarchal blather.

The Way You Taste

Having the taste of how
happy I could be every time
I see your face.
Now that's a beautiful kind
of torture.

TWO HEARTS ONE HOME

My eyes are diamonds, gifted sight baptising sunrise
with scattered moonlight.
Pooled reminiscence rains into waterfalls, bursting
release into bubbled river beds of unknown
excitement.

My mind. Fulfilled dreamscape palettes, painting
moving pictures of summer days in dandelion fields,
planting seeds of memories on to the dog-eared pages
of my poetry books.
pressed periwinkles plant
sleeping permanence
between our final chapter

I looked into your mind and saw our future.
Set to the left of your chestnut eyes I saw me on a
swing always carried upon your
redwood heart.
Reaching forever upwards plucking stars from the noir
to hang from swanned necks

Cut from the same fabric we were delicately
torn from the scriptured cosmos and reformed in
skeletal destiny of marrowed love

Are there days where we can sit on the arms of time
and reflect on the emerald clovers stuffed into our
chest?

We are Weaved into the sacrificial giving of life from
death, preserving nurtured earth as our fingers sew
rebirth, fruitful in expectancy.
Like a babe in arms the heavens will kiss summer
showers onto our perpetually written tomorrow.

Blindfolded anticipation
Brings curled fingers to the tie
Hooded wings reveal nebula eyes
as our smiles touch
The feathered quill traverse's bareness
Press folded mountains onto cupids' crook
And speak words of the flesh in sinful tongues

Unlock hips
Untie my spinal cord
Unravel my spirit
Undo what was whole

Spread it out bare for you
Destiny drips untidy rooms and crumpled pages losing
ourselves in fields of linen
Sculpting arches
Bow
As you
Pluck blush petals with fingers on your poetry hand;
Slickly solving budding riddles to taste her telling tide.
I'll scribe my name upon your glistening scroll with
freshly manicured nails and feed you the harmonies
dipped in honey formed in a glazed throat; Inhale
those three words from my essence and wear it as
cologne
You are summer to my heart and all four seasons to
my soul
As the storms build in clouded eyes
Lighting cracks
Wildfire eyes burn amber
And your flames lick pearl kissed flesh
You smirk catching smoke rings with my ankles
Pertly
Tapping
Morse code into my rib cage
And praying it saves our souls

BUTTERFLY KISSES

His Butterfly kisses,
eyelash wings; protecting the
verdant green orbs that see me.
Really see me.
eyes i will see; eyes I have seen;
in my every lives.

Dipping into your temporal lobe,
bathing in your psych,
time and space to us, limitless.
You are my forever,
yesterday and now.

Massage my heart with your fervor;
keep it warm with the flames ignited,

for only me.
Creating us.

Cupid's arrow dipped in your blood;
now pierced permanently into the organ
bringing me life.
Never to be removed,
or I will be forever lost to you.

Red light moments stolen at every opportunity,
you are the soundtrack to my soul.
Each whisper; I love you,
notes leaving aesthetic chills.
Those goosebump thrills.
Always Longing for your feather touch.

NTITLED

Dappled moonlight
punctured
my hearts darkness

Forest Frolics

Baptise me in the pools of blissful tomorrow's and I will hum to the lullabies sung by the skylarked canopies of our transcendental forest. Walk with me, bare foot through endless rain so we can spill our sensual secrets against the trees. Spread my wings darling dryad, pull my Ivy weaved braids and I will find myself lost in your amethyst eyes; succumbing to mystical energies pooling desperately at my core. The soundtrack to our Luna love dance becomes the rumoured whispers of pretty pixies dancing in the giddy leaves of our here and now.

Emily Willard

CARRY ME IN YOUR WORDS

Dip your fingers into azure starlight
Coat my skin in constellations
Brush my lips in tangerine tendrils formed only by
your tongue
When we are forced apart
fold my soul into a paper crown and adorn it upon
you mind.
Carry me with you inside of a velveteen pouch
Formed in inky swirls pressed into our leather bound
poetry book

Emily Willard

DEPRESSION

I feel you my unbeloved.
Your darkness suffocates me
as it closes in

READ WITH ME

Read with me
The same words
From the same book
Under the same sky
heated by the same sun
Breathing the same air
Thousands of miles apart
longing fills my heart
Pull cords in my core
But it exists solely because
we were allowed to meet
again

Angry Song

Anger
It courses through me like an earthquake
Slow small tremors leading up to something bigger
Teetering on the edge of that unnatural disaster
Feeling like I could tear down buildings if someone,
anyone dares speaks or looks at me the wrong way.

This isn't me
Or who I am
The build up is slow like a adagio
Slow and subtle, it's a long andante in its tempo,

But life
Just life, creates a build up and the tension becomes
more like a crescendo
Filling my Ears and my head with noise coming from
all angles of my being.

Until I explode
Then I become a viper with my words, like venom
filling the veins of my victims

Walls, plates and whatever is in my path of destruction
erupt into pieces
The detonation of my aggravation leaves endless
collateral damage in my frenzied path.

Then it becomes Almost un fixable.
That's when the dust settles and I see through the eyes
of my victims
The guilt drowns me, suffocating in waters I'm not
ready to come out of.

There I'll sleep in the shallows of my self pity and ego
rather than face the music I created.

Emily Willard

THE GREAT ESCAPE

Picturesque promises spread deliciously across the shattered secrets of my soul, pouring creamy melodies of sweet nothings, deceitfully blinding my vision of the needled emotional attack behind your manipulative motives. Akin to bathing on frozen tides, catching heart shaped snowflakes on the tip of my tongue, ignoring the cold burn on stung thighs: numb to the bite until it's too late. With lies like lullabies he composed a tune that sucked on my abandonment filling a hole with sour nothingness, for ever scratching his name on my skull, tainting those forefront memories filling them with court jester complexions. Snatching back the key to the gates of my temple was like cutting the cord with a wooden spoon; determination can be all consuming when you are afraid. He plucked my petals one by one with soft caressing fingers, blinded by his sunbeam smile, wilting over time I was left with nothing but bitter thorns of deceit. My escape; allowed me to tip toe in my flowerless garden, basking in the droplets of spring breaking through the melting snow.

COSTUME CHANGE

The Skin that you see is not a clear representation of
her. That is the gown that she displays for the public
gallery. Those tooth filled grins are painfully clenched;
pinched skin torn between grinding bone. Chest heave
cackles forced to cover her ennui with a sugar sweet
coat of splendour. The children see a flesh dressed
beacon that radiates warmth even when her bones feel
like ice. Warrior paint covers black evidence of her
lack of sleep. Stolen moments behind a locked
bathroom door to disappear into a world of words and
unreachable companions. Her love is chocolate cake
kisses made from painfully broken hands; her calm
facade adroitly hides the fiery temper; a motherly
maestro at icing buns and filling holes in the walls.

It's in the hills of her house that she becomes her
undoing as she reaches inside peeling the layers of
deceit and unbearable discontent. Quickening breaths
clinging to her rib cage her concrete head sways as
oxygen fades. An unsolicited dance that grips her body
each night. Her beacon depletes to a blinking light, as
the final layer of her costume is bled onto the tear-
soaked sheets; Her true self now leaks onto the pages
in prose formed mind spills.

FROZEN GOODBYE

Shattered tusks of frozen glass
Crunch under my weighted feet.
You said goodbye
Walked away
All thats left is my rage
Storm clouds echo your name
Lightning bolts crack from grinding teeth
Mouth begins to thunder
crystalline rivers freeze my eyes shut,
Eternally
Lost to my own elements
Ice crystalline mounds
Of unfettered grief
I unravel, come undone
Cataclysmic destruction to a
Heart so kind
Strangled by inky veins of pain
Caused solely by you.
And the poison last words that
Seeped from your tainted lips.

Not Today

I can feel the tectonic plates shifting in my core, deep physical tremors coming and going with no warning

The oh to familiar sweep of hands unwontedly caressing my skin, this wicked visitor robbing me of all free will

Each breath in, poisonous gas stretching its self out inside of my lungs, digging it's talons into each and every one of my capillaries

Each breath out, ridding me of the precious oxygen that has been replaced, leaving only toxins suffocating me from within.

Every success and achievement of what was; is now

forgotten, as if my brain has been wiped leaving only the thoughts, I have battled so hard to leave behind.

Like a mist, slowly and inevitably turning into a fog
Creeping in, becoming all consuming; I know what's coming I know what is to become of me

This is a road travelled many times before; I will try and drive away from the darkness fighting for the light, but It seems my sword has become blunt and my mind has become weary.

I pray to each and every deity, that the mist doesn't take me today or tomorrow and it allows me to be free; because I don't want to go this time- I just want to be mc.

COLD HAIKU

December moon eyes
Evergreen heart framed with ice
His glacial teeth bite

FIREPLACE

In you I find home.
Yet home feels like an
unreachable destination now.
Lost to the elements and
stolen by the cold.
Knowing my heart will never
be warmed by the fireplace
of my home again.

Emily Willard

NIGHTS QUEEN

Oh Selene so serene
Speckled through the sycamore leaves
The breath of the evening holds in its hands
A stillness coated in sapphire deapth.
A Withdrawn child in nights awning sighs
They tremble in wittering reverence.
Eyes ritually stolen by a velvet cloak with just
Seven stars snared in canopy cracks.
Silent wings glide from bough to ground
Echoed by the night birds calls.
Stepping out bare foot I am claimed by
The magic of Luna and lifted by her grace.
She plants dappled seeds of moonlight
Blossoming into pied piper pathways, drawing me
deeper into Gaia's shadow puppet displays.

A July Evening 2017

Lie with me, drenched in the heated cusp of a July
evening sunshine.
Days surrounded by a plethora of alcoholic beverages
and a pointless picnic we will never come to eat.
As he throws himself onto the soft downy blankets
with an audible thud, I giggle —all man and no grace, I
rolled my eyes.
Here he has arranged our very own hotel room under
the star splattered skies. He pulled me to him, an
unspoken question and a silent reply hung in the air
between us and it tasted delicious.
That first kiss as I sipped from your lips, Bourbon
laced his tongue and all but come undone,
As our tongues touched and danced Smokey spices
infuse my senses , I felt like I could get giddy just from
this kiss.

As he lifted my arms above my head making quick
work with the cotton slip I was wearing, not that it
mattered much it was hardly leaving anything to the
imagination.
He slides adept fingers
S L O W L Y
Up

My
Spine
Right to the base neck, I felt like a spring in my core
coiled up and came to life. My body was betraying me
and I was totally fine with that
With one flip I was on my back.
You rise
Deliberate eyes
Quilted Echos of Hurricane Blues that spoke
everything and nothing all at once.
With one finger he lifts up my chin and whispers into
my ear. Sending

 shivers into what felt like every nerve in my being.
"Look at the sky Emily. Isn't it beautiful?"
Then he drew that finger from my neck at leisurely
pace all the way down to my belly button
Sometimes he didn't even need to touch my skin for
me to feel it, seductive static magic bent at his will.
Anticipation made me high and the tip of his lips gave
away his knowing.
We laid there, lost in each other.
And as if time stood still and allowed us to unfold our

senses and minds, we immortalised that moment in my memories till the moon said it's goodbyes and sun bleached the cover of my favourite night with him.

"Then where?"

Everything seems sort of dull
I have this unshakeable feeling that I don't belong here anymore.
Not like an "I want to end it all" feeling; but, like I want to start now.
Everything just feels mundane for my soul.
I want to experience people
I want to experience life
I want to experience tastes, sounds, feelings, emotions and conversations.
Someone wise said to me "Perhaps we feel so alone because we know what we are truly made of and many don't" and I thought, that's it. Think about it.
You are an outsider looking in what do you see? Go on tell me. Flash floods of dam broken tears pouring from an average face; again.
A smile?
Real?

Can you tell?
do you care either way?
why should you?
you don't know me, overweight, short, painfully
awkward and insecure:
All fickle feelings of a beautifully broken vessel that has
outgrown her body and desperately needs to stretch
out her mind and her soul.
Laying here I feel the pull of the universal plan for me;
like a cord strapped to my core and this life,
belligerently pulling me back by my shoulders. A
guttural ache constantly resides in my stomach. A
burn stinging the back of my nose. A constant itch in
the corners of my eyes. So are those tears that drown
my daily existence are pools of longing?
Puddles of what ifs.
Oceans of distance untraveled.
Just a thought out loud. If I don't belong here
anymore, which way is the way out?

Just thoughts and pondering's of a troubled mind I'm
good :)

Emily Willard

HEAVENLY DEPTHS

Lying with my head under the water.
Silence.
Quiet.
At last.
Coated in the oceans warm embrace.
If only I was brave enough to succumb.
Her seas have always called me home,
Permitting me to drown in its peace instead of my
thoughts,
Sinking; overwhelmed by life ,
Whilst dying of thirst for something more.
I Will submerge myself until peace turns to pain,
Oxygens depleted,
As the water pools into the sockets of my closed eyes.
At that moment, I force them wide until my lenses
burn,
Breaking her waters with a life saving breath,
As much as I love the silence in the depth of her
shores.
I chose to leave her behind,
Reminding me that I choose to live every time

Emily Willard

Mind's Sky

Stars of whimsical
imagination hang from her
mind's sky

DAVE

Him- I see a rainbow and
dissect it
Her- I see a rainbow and
open it right up

A Fairytale for Big Kids

A COLLABORATION: EMILY WILLARD & LISEA SILVERS

Startled storms trip over forced laughterous thunder building within the iris of the clown.

[[gusts start to chatter and whisper about a sweet girl who doesn't understand how often the sky can hold you with one hand, while the other breaks a branch]]

A dance with the skyline finds a child with a head made of clouds, feet formed in weighted
Ore.

[[The breath of a chanting boy falls upon stagnant ears, can i pull him in?]]

A cordial contradiction of sorts
// Nothing will be set in stone for something so breezy.

Oakwood rings encircle the lily pad palms of a potter forming the hips to a song he's been humming for centuries
- restless cherub wings tickling a giraffes throat, harps pulling petals off daisy's
(loves me, loves me not, loves) ,
a stumbling fawn tip toeing into leaves continuously

 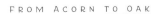

falling so they never land on the dreams of tomorrow.

(((DID YOU KNOW THE JERICHO FLOWER NEVER DIES? THAT REMINDS ME : HAVE YOU EVER SAT AND WATCHED A ROSE SAY GOODBYE? DELICATE IN ITS DEMISE, THE WRINKLES ON THE EDGE OF THE BLOOM AS THE PIGMENT BLEEDS AND DRIES FROM THE OUT LEAVING DYE FROM THE SUN STILL RICH IN THE CENTER OF ITS HEART. I ASK, ONLY SO YOU KNOW.

IT'S HOW I WISH TO FADE INTO THE DARKNESS : HOW I CAME INTO THE LIGHT.))

A skipping stone tapping along a frozen gorge// sings to the throats of winged fish

((DO WE MAKE UP WORDS AS WE GO ALONG?))

The secrets of the deep are harmonised from the first breath of the ocean whistled from the river mouth, ending in a roar to the seasoned permanence of bodied emotion.

Rusted iron toes dipped in the final resting place of April

She knew her melancholy month would be followed by a tittering of bluebells and the gloves of foxes. The sobriety of a pathless wood makes way for Petel headed wildlings.

Perfect hats for tiny mice.

//If a tree grows in the woods and no one is around to see it,
will it still stand with Grace? /

[[the flower with the white hair pens poetry
with her stems.

a nurtured growth birthed from a maternal shift.]]

((I FIND MOST PEOPLE WHO HAVE SEEN THE FLAMES UP
CLOSE ARE THE ONES WHO GIVE OVER PORCELAIN WITHOUT
NEEDING A WATCH. HER GIFT WAS A SWORD DRUM THAT
PLAYED BEATS OF WAR AGAINST - THE DARK KNIGHT.))

elk horns elegantly echo rabbit heart songs
         - badum badum badum -
as they settle on to downy spruced earth, giggling roots
prepared to tuck them in.
     elder woods hush their bark and wolves hiccup on
howls under direction from a conductor moon, a
baton of nova tapping on the shoulder of the great
bear resting on her shores.
         Pirouettes of whispers drift on waves born
from long forgotten ships sailing the sky - elysian
canvas bearing the seal of Orion.

[[Shapes in the midnight clouds form animals only we know, as we count the stars from the ground up, no longer wondering if the angels envy our view.]]

Nightingales painted in dresses of longing stick twelve shiny pins into birthed Braeburn.

((WAITING FOR HIS RETURN))

A Cuckoo - coos to the old ones and weaves its feathers into the wings of smaller fowl.

-Lifting them up one by one to the cornflower stepping stones coating evermore-

Within the Way of Milk, a crescent growl shatters the void of sound to create a nook in the exultations of space where a singular hope could rest -

We are only as brave as the soul we serve and we are the many - nay, the few - who danced beneath a luminescent faith. A belief in souls traveling across time to see how it all ends.

WE ARE THE INFINITE PROMISE OF A BEGGING TO UNDERSTAND HOW WE COULD BE THE LUCKY ONES

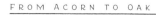

SEPTEMBER SADNESS

September clings onto the last of summer's embrace
and holds onto hollow fruitless evenings.
Reminiscing of sunsets spent with him.
I can't help but lie in aching wait for the night to creep
in, shadowing low leaden days spent without being
held tightly together.
Clementine skies with peppermint claws makes me feel
alive.
Can you miss something you have never really had?
Times toes step into another three hundred and sixty-
five pirouettes and wraps my hands in silken ties of
hope. Praying for the space between us to be
Obliterated, fragments of
"Who knows, but let's try" floating into the nether.
The darkened vibrations of my soul sing towards the
liquid luminescence of my heart: so, he can always
find his way.

But he ceases to come.
The day must have gotten lost because it never arrived.
A thousand mornings held inside, a butterfly trapped inside of a hurricane humming melodies of absolution.
Whistle moth wing dust of my lungs and hear my wanton cries.
Midnight memories have me catching whispers in the dark confinements of my room, so I rise with cotton wool between my molars.
I need to pull the moon into me on a lasso, locking onyx thoughts out of my dreams.
Come with me as I Step into my woodland slumber
Because beneath the trees I find blissful sanctum.
So please just wake me up, when September ends.

Emily Willard

A Few of My Favourite Things

Morning cuddles from the lights of my life, equally paired with the sleepy final cuddly goodnites at bedtime.

Taking the lead off my dogs collar in overgrown summer meadows, watching her freely bound into babbling brooks with her staffy smile painted across her face.

My mother's laugh, high pitched and pure. Exploding from a normally quiet and reserved beautiful lady. So deeply contagious, I am smiling just at the thought of her being happy.

Music, especially the type that makes you cry. A playlist named for each emotion and ones you share with friends.

Then, there is crying itself. That emotional release in all its forms, proving to me I am in fact human after all.

His smile and the way it commands his eyes to follow
suit and what it does to my core each time they pair
up.
First kisses and memories of them. Awkward angles
and butterfly sighs. Anticipation bubbling through my
veins as a "potential" tries to break the surface.
Trees, thinking of all they have seen and the secrets
they breathe, they resemble real magic
to me.
Summer dinners, cold meats and salads, finger picked
in the garden in playful intervals.
My children's laughter, infectious yo everyone lucky
enough to witness such joy.
Winter nights wrapped up in blankets "like sausage
rolls", hugged by the scent of cinnamon and slow
cooked stews.

Emily Willard

ᎩOU ᎫNOW ᎹHO ᎩOU ᎪRE

To the ones I feel setting fires in my mind, stoking the
embers in my darkened skies.
To the ones I hold close as they ignite the blaze long
extinguished.

To the ones pouring love into my heart just as it was
giving up.

To the ones that wrap balmy tendrils around
emotionally open wounds.
The vibrancy of my once burnt aura now glows
Solaris yellow, resting like a sunflower head. Tilted
back bathing in your ever sun lightened existence.
You know who you are,
I hand vibrant thank-yous out in blooming bouquets
freshly picked from the evergreen gardens of my
nurtured heart.

Emily Willard

THE RISE OF FALL

Summers fade like Polaroids
Wilting at its burnt edges curling at
The cool caress of Septembers
Fingers.
Conducting the seasons with a flick of its wrist.
Mottled horizons bring forth the timely death of blue
skies, with huddled warmth of Sols highs.
The willows weep Kelly tears as it's limbs are dragged
into the breeze like a wailing child reaching fervently
for its mother.
Jade tresses suffocate silently beneath burnt crimson,
red fox rugs.
But in the fall of a season comes the rise of Fall.

Autumn delicately pirouettes in carnival colours and is
ready for centre stage at the ball.
Trees shimmy and shake dancing leaves from branch
to ground, with very little subtlety the Earth becomes a
fanfare of playground.
Which elms creak and reach in billowing ballets as
hurricanes pull rainbows from the skies playing hoopla
with fallen coats. Whispered breaths promise drawn in
even evenings. under hallow skies.
Flamed foliage paint jewels upon the oaks cloak while
Horse Chestnuts drop their spikes crowns.
Gold and scarlet adorns the Earth and paints it regal.
Such a Buoyant affair of seasonal flare.
To bid the summer Adieu

Emily Willard

JOURNAL ENTRY NOVEMBER 2020

If I could steal a moment in time, I would pull the notes you sang to me from your throat that morning, drape myself on your chest and play them on repeat. "Give me a minute to hold my girl' Weaved into my soul along with the smell you left upon your pillow the day you walked away. Your smell, earthy and always with a tinge of sweat, but that scent was sent from the gods as a gift just for me. I sometimes; while reading, catch myself slowly running my thumb across the top of my ear. just like you would subconsciously while we watched a film or talked to friends on those garden evenings. Some days it make me smile. Others it leaves an empty sick feeling along side breaths that seem to have never belonged inside of my aching chest. I look upon the woman in the mirror, wiping tears from a hollowed out skull. Scooped out "forever" moments, and blackened eyes adorned from sleep avoidance. Bumping into you with closed eyes always ends in

aching pools of what was, and leaves a bitter taste on my tongue of what is now. Cracked open and yet another piece of my heart resides almost definitely in their bin. If I give you the way through my steel ribcage, know that you will always reside along side the breaths in my chest. You repulse me and I love you and that needs to end. I hear your Motorbike every day visiting our next door neighbour and the dog goes wild knowing it's you. Not Once walking past our house have you said Hi. 6 years. Ended on good terms, but I'm starting to realise you are not a good person. Sadly another old chapter of a story unfinished.

Time to open my book and start from scratch.

Once upon a time. Emily learned that she made for great company and found a world where her people belonged. Guess what. She hasn't looked back!

RESURRECTION

Four angels mimicking the ocean waves flashed
incandescent light in to the throats of their suitors,
Plucking sunflowers, from the sockets of Gaia they
place them in the empty ribcages of the dead.
With dandelion wish breaths the hearts bloom from
the shattered wombs of deception.
A gust of wind explodes slicing through frozen silence.
The angels hold strings to their chosen and scratch a
shoreline with their puppeteer claws.
The only way to save dismal disgrace is to raise their
forsaken foe once more.

IT'S EASIER NOW

And if I were to break again.
It's easier now.
Because you will always hold
my heart and pull me back
"That mirror game is
strong"

COURAGEOUS LOVE

Love blindly
Love courageously
Love recklessly
Love intently
Love vibrantly
Love consciously
Love Wholly
Love wildly
Love gracefully
Love independently
Love selflessly
Love gently
Love brightly
Love passionately
Love hungrily
Love adamantly
Love boldly
Love loudly
Love beautifully
Most of all
LOVE FREELY

Emily Willard

ABOUT EMILY

Emily Willard was born in Wiltshire England.
Growing up she always loved to read, and though she
never quite finished school that didn't stop her from
wanting to learn.

After becoming lost for a while becoming a mother
unlocked her creativity once more, writing stories and
creating art for or alongside her children.

Journaling has always been important to her especially
in more recent years where she has really picked up on
sharing her life through her writing.

Emily loves writing short stories and poetry and feels a
deep magnetism to anything ethereal.

There is nothing more that she loves to do than losing
herself in a good book. Especially if it transports her
to another realm with the fae, witches and monsters.

From Acorn to Oak is her first collection of poetry
exploring her heart and soul as well as her love for
storytelling.

STAY CONNECTED

Instagram:
  @em.wpoetry
  @soul_connection_poets

Facebook
  Em.wpoetry

Made in the USA
Coppell, TX
29 March 2022